Computer Coding with Scratch 3.0 Workbook

Written by

Craig Steele

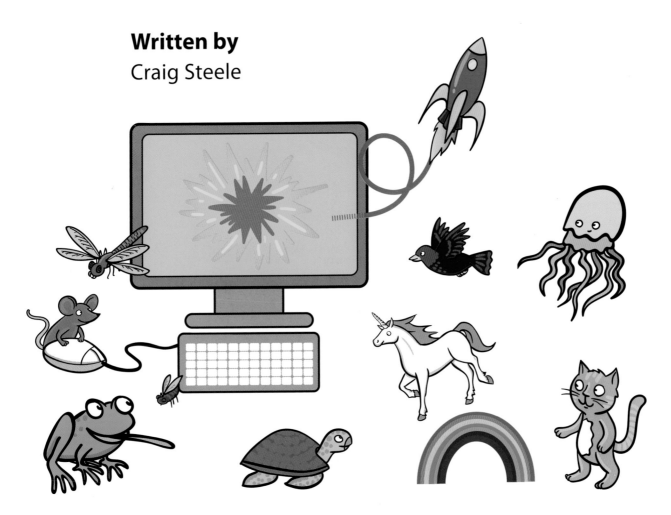

DK | Penguin Random House

Written by Craig Steele
Editors Kathleen Teece, Abhijit Dutta
US Editor Margaret Parrish
Senior Editors Shannon Beatty, Roohi Sehgal
Designer Peter Radcliffe
Project Art Editor Kanika Kalra
Illustrator Katie Knutton
Jacket Coordinator Issy Walsh
Jacket Designer Dheeraj Arora
DTP Designer Sachin Gupta
Project Picture Researcher Sakshi Saluja
Managing Editors Laura Gilbert, Monica Saigal
Deputy Managing Art Editor Ivy Sengupta
Managing Art Editor Diane Peyton Jones
Pre-production Producer David Almond
Producer Basia Ossowska
Delhi Team Head Malavika Talukder
Creative Director Helen Senior
Publishing Director Sarah Larter

First American Edition, 2019
Published in the United States by DK Publishing
1450 Broadway, Suite 801, New York, NY 10018

Scratch is a project of the Lifelong Kindergarten Group at the
MIT Media Lab. See http://scratch.mit.edu

Picture Credits
**The publisher would like to thank the following for their kind
permission to reproduce their photographs:**
(Key: c-center; l-left; r-right)
5 **ESA / Hubble:** NASA, Hubble Heritage Team (ca).
7 **ESA / Hubble:** NASA, Hubble Heritage Team (crb). 8 **ESA / Hubble:** NASA,
Hubble Heritage Team (c). 12 **ESA / Hubble:** NASA, Hubble Heritage Team (cr).
16 **Dreamstime.com:** Lemonadv (c). 30 **Dreamstime.com:** Forplayday (c).

All other images © Dorling Kindersley
For further information see: www.dkimages.com

DK books are available at special discounts when purchased
in bulk for sales promotions, premiums, fund-raising, or
educational use. For details, contact: DK Publishing Special Markets,
1450 Broadway, Suite 801, New York, NY 10018
SpecialSales@dk.com

Printed and bound in China

A WORLD OF IDEAS:
SEE ALL THERE IS TO KNOW

www.dk.com

I prefer Scratch to scratching furniture!

I still think it should have been called Pinch!

Contents

My coding is going swimmingly.

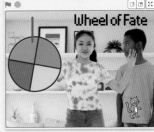
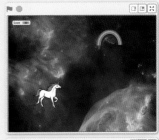

What is Scratch?

Scratch is a creative tool you can use to build your own games, interactive stories, music, and art. You use Scratch to write computer code—this is a list of instructions that the computer will follow to bring your idea to life.

What you'll learn
• What kinds of Scratch projects you can make
• What tools are built in
• What the ingredients of a Scratch project are

Visual programming

You create Scratch projects using a visual programming language. This means that rather than having to type the code (the instructions), you use blocks of code that you snap together to create your projects. This makes it easier to get started.

Sprites

Games and stories wouldn't be very interesting without characters. Scratch's characters are called sprites. There is a sprite library full of them to use!

Scratch program

Code is put together to make a set of instructions, called a program. You can use different blocks in a Scratch program to make a sprite fly around, laugh out loud, and react to other sprites.

Cat's my name!

A cat is the default sprite, which means it's always there at the start.

READ ME!

This book is based on **Scratch 3.0**, the latest version of Scratch at the time of writing. The games won't work on older versions, so make sure you have 3.0. **See page 40 for details of how to get Scratch.**

Coding blocks

Different types of blocks have different colors. You'll learn what kind of things these do later.

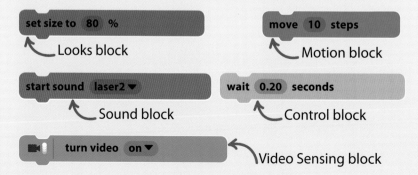

set size to 80 %
Looks block

move 10 steps
Motion block

start sound laser2 ▼
Sound block

wait 0.20 seconds
Control block

turn video on ▼
Video Sensing block

What makes up a Scratch project?

Here's a Scratch project. It's a little like a play. The action takes place in an area called the stage. The "actors" (the sprites) are controlled by lists of "instructions" (the code). Behind is the backdrop, which can be changed.

Click here to stop the code from running.

The flag runs (starts) the code in your project.

Score 30

Scoreboard

Code is used to control each sprite. It can make them move, change size, talk, and more.

You can add backdrops from the backdrop library or make your own.

Libraries

Scratch comes packed with fun characters, spectacular backdrops, and interesting sound effects you can use in your projects. If that isn't enough—you can even use the tools in Scratch to make your own. Let your imagination soar— you'll soon pick up the coding skills you need!

Right-clicking

During Scratch projects you might need to right-click on your computer mouse. If your mouse has one button instead of two, you can hold down the control (CTRL/ctrl) or shift key (⇧) on your keyboard as you click.

A world of projects

Scratch can bring all kinds of ideas to life. The Explore section of the Scratch website contains lots of projects made by other people. It's time to see what you can do.

Let's start coding!

Using Scratch

Learn what some of the most important parts of Scratch do on these pages. Come back to these pages if you can't find where something is during a project.

What you'll learn
• The different areas of Scratch
• The different Scratch tools for building projects

Pick your language here.

Save projects to your computer and start new ones under File.

Select the Code tab to build the code.

Use the Costumes tab to change how sprites look.

You can add new sounds to sprites here.

This is where you'll find the code blocks. They're divided by type of block into sections.

This icon (picture) takes you to a menu of extensions. These are extra blocks you can add to the code area.

This area can be used to store helpful code blocks, to use again in other projects.

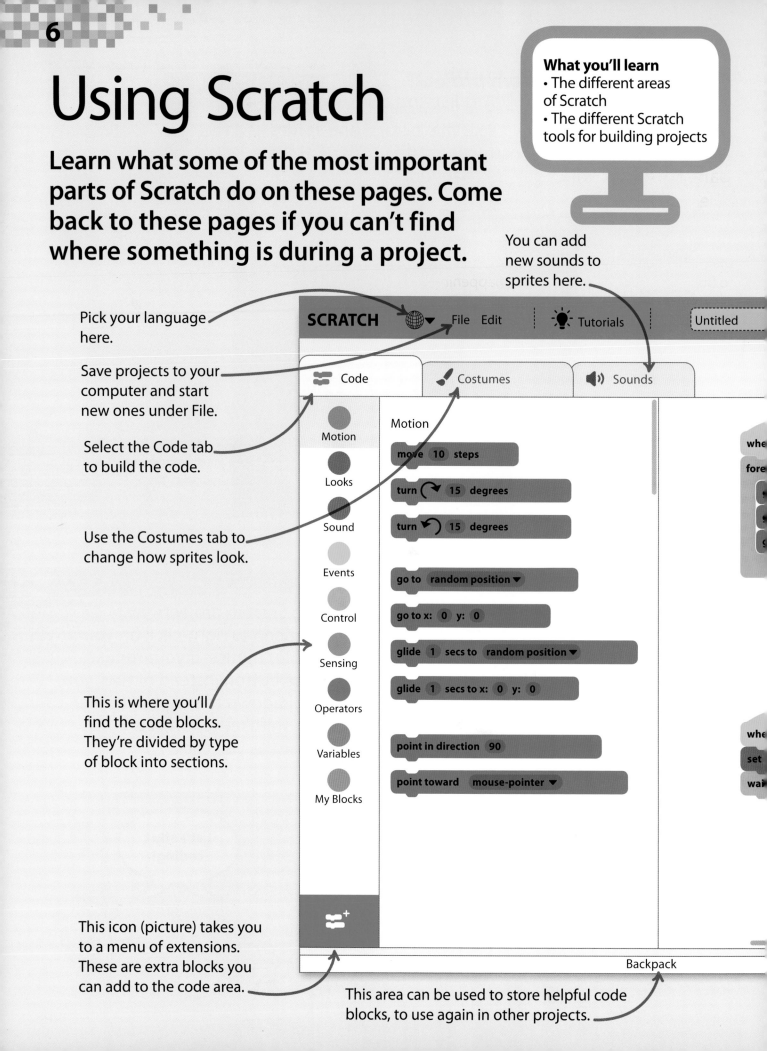

SCRATCH   File   Edit   Tutorials   Untitled

Code   Costumes   Sounds

Motion

Motion

move 10 steps

turn 15 degrees

turn 15 degrees

Looks

Sound

go to random position ▼

Events

go to x: 0 y: 0

Control

glide 1 secs to random position ▼

Sensing

glide 1 secs to x: 0 y: 0

Operators

point in direction 90

Variables

point toward mouse-pointer ▼

My Blocks

Backpack

▶ Map of the Scratch editor

You'll find sprites in the sprites list and backdrops (backgrounds) in the stage list. Coding blocks are found in the blocks palette and put together in the code area. The project appears in the stage area.

| BLOCKS PALETTE | CODE AREA | STAGE AREA |
| SPRITES LIST |
| BACKPACK | STAGE LIST |

The code area is where you drag blocks and join them to build your code.

When you run your Scratch project, you'll see the action happening here on the stage.

Click here to make your project full screen.

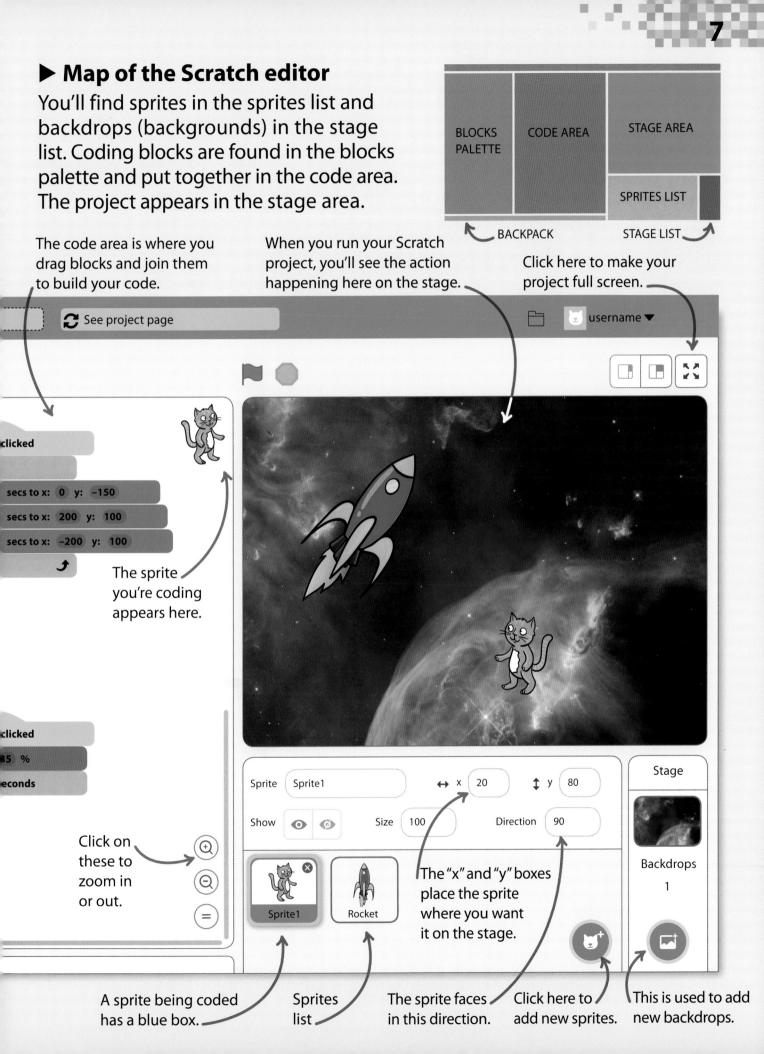

⟳ See project page

username ▼

The sprite you're coding appears here.

clicked

secs to x: 0 y: −150

secs to x: 200 y: 100

secs to x: −200 y: 100

clicked

85 %

seconds

Click on these to zoom in or out.

Sprite Sprite1 ↔ x 20 ↕ y 80

Show 👁 🚫 Size 100 Direction 90

The "x" and "y" boxes place the sprite where you want it on the stage.

Sprite1 Rocket

Stage

Backdrops 1

A sprite being coded has a blue box.

Sprites list

The sprite faces in this direction.

Click here to add new sprites.

This is used to add new backdrops.

Unicorn Rush

Have you ever dreamed of making a computer game? Now's your chance with this Scratch project! Follow the simple steps to make a space unicorn game, which is a race against the clock to collect rainbows.

What you'll learn
• How to add new sprites
• How to control sprites
• How to use forever loops
• How to add collectibles to games
• How to add variables such as score

A score box keeps track of the rainbows you collect.

The rainbows appear in random places around the screen.

Score 30

Use the arrow keys on your keyboard to move the unicorn up, down, left, and right.

The nebula backdrop shows a cloud of dust and gas in space.

▲ What you do

The unicorn is controlled by pressing the arrow keys. Every time the unicorn collects a rainbow, 10 points are added to the player's score. After 10 seconds the game ends. Try to beat your score the next time you play!

1 Getting started

Let's start a brand-new project. Open Scratch and click on **File** at the top left of the screen. Choose **New** from the drop-down menu to start a blank project.

2 Bye for now, Scratch Cat

The Scratch Cat sprite is there at the start of every project, but we don't need it for this game. Delete Scratch Cat by right-clicking on the cat icon in the sprites list at the bottom right of Scratch and choosing **delete**.

3 Adding a new sprite

Let's introduce the hero of the game. Add a new sprite by clicking on the **Choose a Sprite** icon at the bottom right. Type "Unicorn" into the search bar of the sprite library. Click the "Unicorn Running" sprite to add it to your sprite list.

4 Renaming sprites

Renaming a sprite makes it easier to understand your code. Make sure you've clicked on the sprite in the list, then click the text box in the information panel. Use your keyboard to type the new name—let's change it to "Unicorn." The sprite has now been renamed.

5 Resizing sprites

The Unicorn looks great, but it's a bit too big for this project. You can use the information panel to change the size of a sprite. Change the size to 50 for this game.

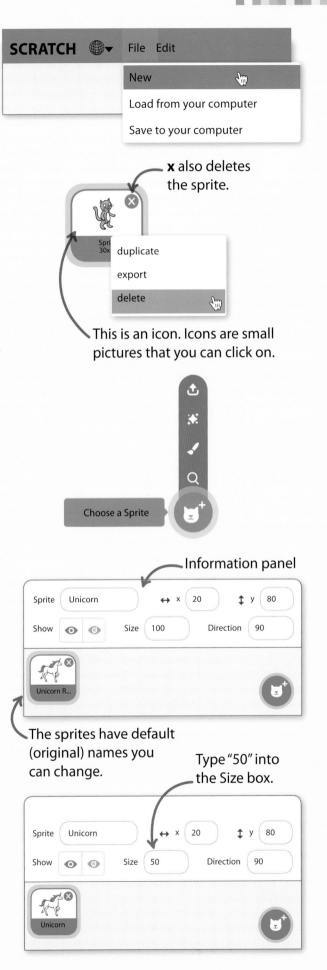

x also deletes the sprite.

This is an icon. Icons are small pictures that you can click on.

Choose a Sprite

Information panel

The sprites have default (original) names you can change.

Type "50" into the Size box.

6 Coding the sprite

Now let's add some code blocks so the player can control the Unicorn. You'll need to head over to the **Code** tab at the top left of Scratch to do this. The **when flag clicked** block is the first one you need. You'll find it by clicking on the yellow **Events** section. Drag the block into the code area to add it to your code.

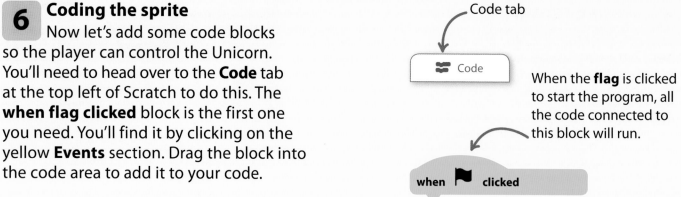

Code tab

Code

When the **flag** is clicked to start the program, all the code connected to this block will run.

when ⚑ clicked

7 Making it move

Now carefully add the blocks below. When you place the blocks next to each other they will snap together. You'll need to look in the sections called **Events**, **Motion**, **Control**, and **Sensing** to find them. Look for each block in the section that matches its color—you'll find them much easier that way.

Running a program

Computer coders talk about running code, or running a program—don't worry, no exercise is involved. It just means starting the program you've coded. In Scratch, you run your program when you click on the **flag**.

If you add the wrong block, you can delete it by right-clicking on it and choosing **Delete Block**.

The code inside a **forever** block repeats while the program is running. This is called a forever loop.

The Unicorn will point toward the right.

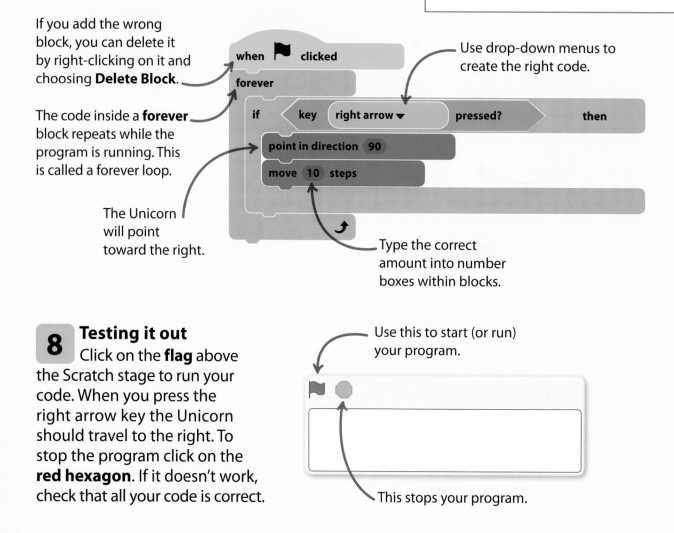

when ⚑ clicked
forever
  if < key right arrow ▼ pressed? > then
    point in direction 90
    move 10 steps

Use drop-down menus to create the right code.

Type the correct amount into number boxes within blocks.

8 Testing it out

Click on the **flag** above the Scratch stage to run your code. When you press the right arrow key the Unicorn should travel to the right. To stop the program click on the **red hexagon**. If it doesn't work, check that all your code is correct.

Use this to start (or run) your program.

This stops your program.

9 Moving in every direction

Great! The Unicorn moves—but it only goes in one direction. Add some extra code that lets it move in other directions. The new blocks are similar to your previous code, but this time the Unicorn will point in a different direction based on the arrow key you press.

Aim to get the code right!

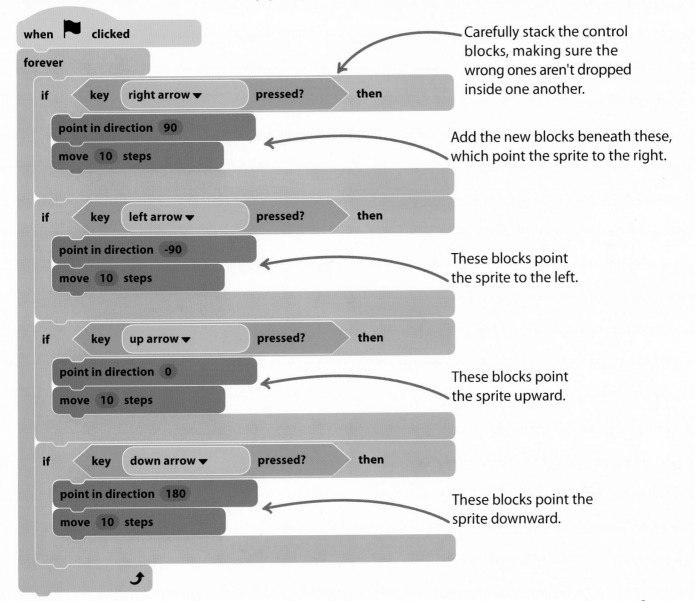

Carefully stack the control blocks, making sure the wrong ones aren't dropped inside one another.

Add the new blocks beneath these, which point the sprite to the right.

These blocks point the sprite to the left.

These blocks point the sprite upward.

These blocks point the sprite downward.

```
when 🚩 clicked
forever
  if key right arrow ▾ pressed? then
    point in direction 90
    move 10 steps

  if key left arrow ▾ pressed? then
    point in direction -90
    move 10 steps

  if key up arrow ▾ pressed? then
    point in direction 0
    move 10 steps

  if key down arrow ▾ pressed? then
    point in direction 180
    move 10 steps
```

10 More testing

Test your code again. Click on the **flag** and then try moving the Unicorn around the screen using the arrow keys. If your code isn't working as expected, don't panic. Look carefully to see if you can see any mistakes.

11 Spotting a bug!

Our code is working, but there is something strange going on. When you press the up arrow key the Unicorn flips upside down. It still works—but it looks a bit strange. Computer programmers call a mistake or problem with their code a "bug."

Help!

12 Let's fix it!

We can add in some code to fix this bug. Add the **set rotation style** block to the top of your code blocks, right after the **when flag clicked** block. You'll find this block in the **Motion** section. This keeps the Unicorn facing the right way up.

You will need to separate the blocks and put the new block in between.

13 Setting the scene

Our Unicorn can now whizz upward, downward, left, and right. Now, let's make the project look more exciting by changing the backdrop. Use the **Choose a Backdrop** menu at the bottom right. Search for one called "Nebula" and click on it to make the unicorn look like it's in space.

Click on the backdrop icon in the stage list section.

14 Collectibles

Many games have special objects that are collected by the hero, called collectibles. These might be jewels or coins. In our game, the Unicorn is obsessed with rainbows. These collectibles are actually sprites. Use the **Choose a Sprite** menu again and search for the "Rainbow" sprite. Click on it to add it to your project.

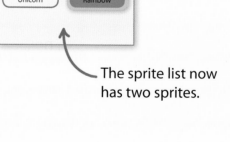

The sprite list now has two sprites.

15 Resizing the Rainbow

This new sprite is the wrong size. Change the size to 50 in the information panel.

Type "50" into the Size box.

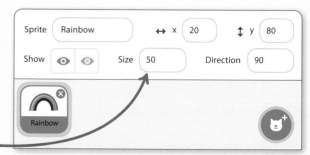

16 Placing the Rainbow

Next, we need to make sure the Rainbow appears when the game starts. We will use code to make this a random position that the player won't expect. It would be boring if the Rainbow appeared in the same place each time! Click on the Rainbow sprite in the sprites list and then add these blocks.

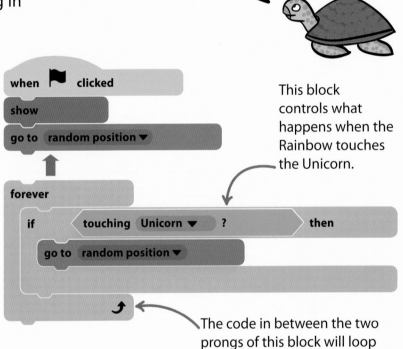

```
when [flag] clicked
show
go to  random position ▼
```

17 Random positions

Now try clicking the **flag** over and over. You should see the Rainbow appearing in different positions on the stage.

18 Collecting rainbows

Let's add some code to the Rainbow sprite that lets the Unicorn collect it. This code means that the Rainbow will vanish when the Unicorn touches it and appear again elsewhere on the screen. The **forever** block means this will keep happening over and over again while the project is running.

```
when [flag] clicked
show
go to  random position ▼

forever
   if <  touching  Unicorn ▼  ? > then
      go to  random position ▼
```

That's turtally random!

This block controls what happens when the Rainbow touches the Unicorn.

The code in between the two prongs of this block will loop around and run forever.

19 Nearly there

Try running your program now. You should be able to fly around as the Unicorn, collecting rainbows! This version of the game never ends—so you could keep collecting rainbows all day.

20 Keeping score

Keeping track of the player's score is an important feature in games. To do this you need to create a variable. Click on the orange **Variables** section and choose **Make a Variable**. Type "Score" to name the variable.

New Variable   ✕

New variable name:

Score

○ For all sprites   ○ For this sprite only

Cancel   OK

21 Updating the score

Now add these extra code blocks to the code for the Rainbow sprite. This will update the score every time the player collects a rainbow. Remember to choose "Score" from the drop-down menu in the variable blocks.

Easy!

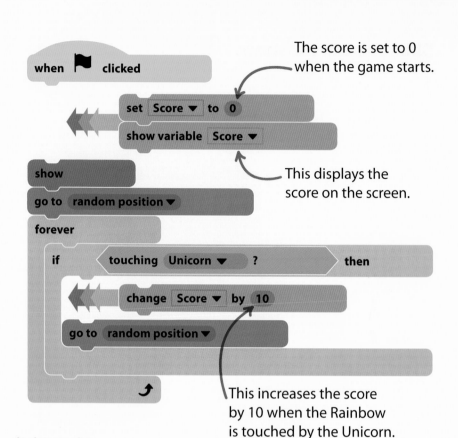

The score is set to 0 when the game starts.

```
when [flag] clicked
set Score ▼ to 0
show variable Score ▼
show
go to random position ▼
forever
    if < touching Unicorn ▼ ? > then
        change Score ▼ by 10
        go to random position ▼
```

This displays the score on the screen.

This increases the score by 10 when the Rainbow is touched by the Unicorn.

22 Does it work?

Try running your project by clicking the **flag**. Check that the score goes up when you collect rainbows. Excellent—you've almost finished. Remember, if something isn't working, go back and look at your code carefully. You might spot a typing mistake or see that you've put a block in the wrong place.

Check for typing errors!

23 Using a timer

Scratch has a built-in timer that you can use in your games. In this game, let's use it to count how many seconds have passed since the game started. You can add this code to your Rainbow sprite to stop the game after 10 seconds.

```
when timer ▼ > 10
    loudness
  ✓ timer
```

Choose **timer** from the drop-down menu

```
when timer ▼ > 10
hide
stop all ▼
```

These blocks will run when the timer counts past 10 seconds.

This hides the sprite, so no more rainbows can be collected.

This block stops all code from running.

24 Play it!

That's it! You've completed your first game. You've already used some of the most important blocks in Scratch, including **forever** loops, **if** blocks, and **variables**. Don't worry if you don't understand how it all works yet—you'll figure it out more with each new game.

Show what you know

1. Circle the correct words in bold in each sentence.

1a. A **sprite** / **pixie** can move around the stage. It is controlled by **magic** / **code** blocks.

1b. A **backdrop** / **background** is used to set the scene for each project.

2. The score is set to 0. What is the value of the score if these blocks are run?

`change Score ▼ by 5`   Score is ....

`change Score ▼ by -2`   Score is ....

`change Score ▼ by (1 + 9)`   Score is ....

3. Which number should go in the empty window to make the sprite move to the right if the right arrow key is pressed?

```
when [flag] clicked
forever
  if < key right arrow ▼ pressed? > then
    point in direction ( )
    move 10 steps
```

0   90   180   270   Circle the correct answer.

4. Which block would you change to make the game last longer?

....

5. What would happen if you change the number in the **move steps** block to 20? ....

6. Which is the correct block to use to stop the Unicorn from turning upside down? ....

Challenge! Change the code so the Unicorn moves slower around the stage.

Wheel of Fate

This is a multiplayer game of chance—use your hand to spin the wheel and if it lands on your color, you lose the game! What will your forfeit be? This project will teach you to use the Scratch 3.0 paint editor and video motion feature.

What you'll learn
• How to use the paint editor
• How to add video motion

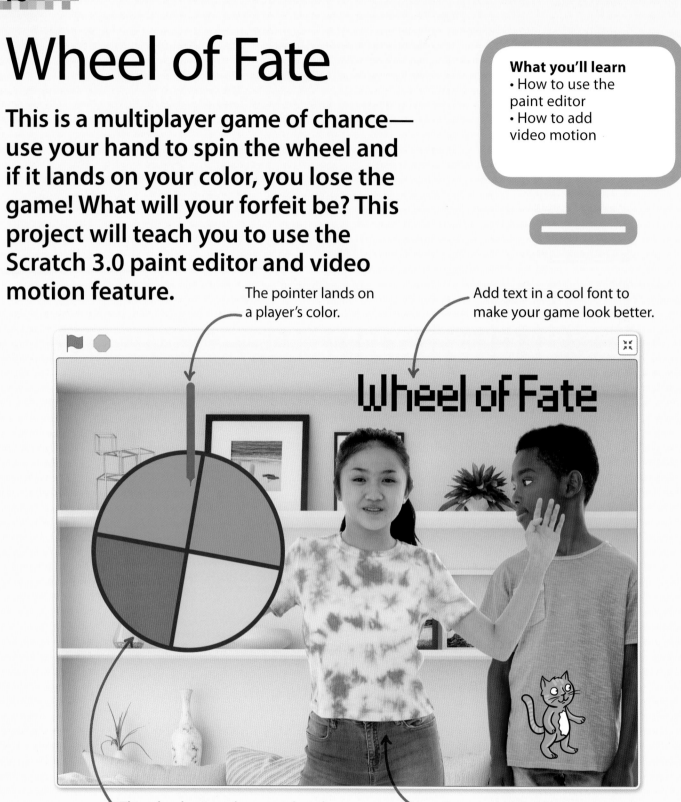

The pointer lands on a player's color.

Add text in a cool font to make your game look better.

The wheel spins when your hand "touches" it in the live video.

Put yourself in the game with the video feature!

▲ What you do

Each player picks a color. When your hand is touching the wheel on the video it starts to spin. Each spin is random—so you can't predict where the pointer will land. Once the spinning stops, Scratch Cat announces the color. You could make that person do a forfeit, such as stand on one leg.

1 A new project

Start a new blank project and let's begin. Scratch Cat is the presenter for this project. The Cat sprite is added to the project automatically so you don't need to do anything. Add this code to the Cat sprite to place it at the bottom right of the stage when the project starts.

2 Edit the backdrops

Backdrops are used to set the scene for projects. For this project, you will create your own backdrop. First, select the **Stage** section at the bottom right corner of Scratch.

Stage

Backdrops
1

```
when 🏳 clicked
go to x: 150 y: -125
```

← You'll find this block in the **Motion** section.

3 Next, click on the **Backdrops** tab at the top left of Scratch. This opens the paint editor.

The paint editor is great for making your own backdrops and sprites. It might look complicated at first, but don't worry—you don't need to know how to use it all right away.

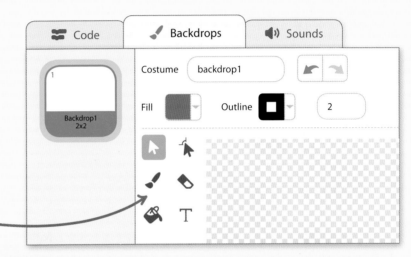

Coordinates

We use a pair of numbers called x–y coordinates to position a sprite. These are added into the Scratch code. The x coordinate pinpoints how far left or right the sprite is across the stage. The y coordinate shows how far up or down it is. Coordinates start small at the left or bottom and get bigger if the sprite is farther right or up. Wheel of Fate uses coordinates to position Scratch Cat at the bottom right.

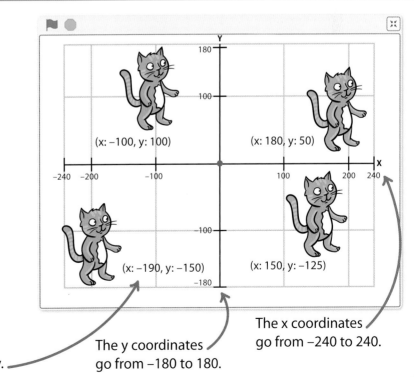

The x coordinate comes before the y.

The y coordinates go from –180 to 180.

The x coordinates go from –240 to 240.

4 Adding text

Let's add a title. Click on the **Text** tool. This tool lets you add words to the image. Click on the main painting area and then type the title of the project: "Wheel of Fate."

Click here to choose the **Text** tool.

5 Change the color

Click on the **Fill** icon to bring up a tool called **color picker**. By moving the sliders you can choose the exact color you want. Pick your favorite color for the title text.

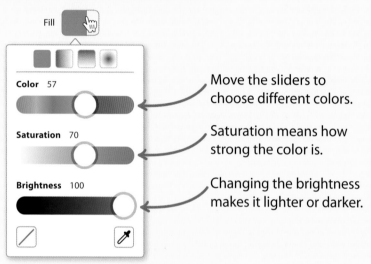

Move the sliders to choose different colors.

Saturation means how strong the color is.

Changing the brightness makes it lighter or darker.

6 Fancy fonts

The paint editor also lets you choose different fonts for your text. These change the way the text looks. Click on the drop-down menu and you'll see a list of different choices.

Pick a font you like the look of. "Pixel" looks great for this project.

7 Move and resize it

Next, move the title so it is at the top right of the backdrop and make it bigger. Use the **Select** tool to move the text by dragging it to the right place and dropping it there. To change the size, drag the dots around the text outward.

Click here to choose the **Select** tool.

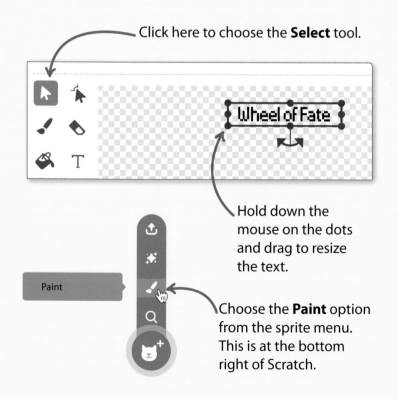

Hold down the mouse on the dots and drag to resize the text.

8 Make the wheel

Now it's time to create a new sprite for the spinning wheel. Draw your own sprite by choosing the **Paint** icon from the **Choose a Sprite** menu. Rename it as "Wheel."

Choose the **Paint** option from the sprite menu. This is at the bottom right of Scratch.

Make sure **Outlined** is selected so the circle's middle isn't filled in.

Undo button

9 Draw a circle

First, click on the **Convert to Bitmap** button. Now, select the **Circle** tool. Click and drag to draw the circle. Hold down the **Shift Key** (⇧) while drawing to make it a perfect circle. A crosshair icon (⊕) shows where the middle of the screen is. Position the circle with the crosshair in the middle so it's center stage. Click **Undo** if you go wrong.

The **Circle** tool is for drawing circles and ovals.

Drag the circle by the edge to move it around.

First press the **Convert to Bitmap** button.

10 Slice and fill the circle

Use the **Line** tool to cut the circle into sections. Draw a straight line by clicking and dragging it from one side of the circle to the other. Use the **Fill** tool to color each section. Choose a color and click in a section to fill it.

Line tool

Fill tool

Make sure there are no gaps at the edges.

11 One more sprite

You need one more sprite for this project. This is an arrow that will point at the wheel to show which section is chosen. Add a sprite using the **Choose a Sprite** menu. Find the sprite called "Arrow1." Click on it to add it to your sprite list.

"Arrow1" can be found in the sprite library.

12 Delete the extra costumes

Each sprite can have different costumes, or looks. Click on the Arrow1 sprite in the sprite list, then click on the **Costumes** tab at the top left of Scratch. You'll see a list of different costumes. We only need the third one (the arrow pointing down). Remove the other costumes by right-clicking on them and choosing **delete**.

Delete the extra costumes.

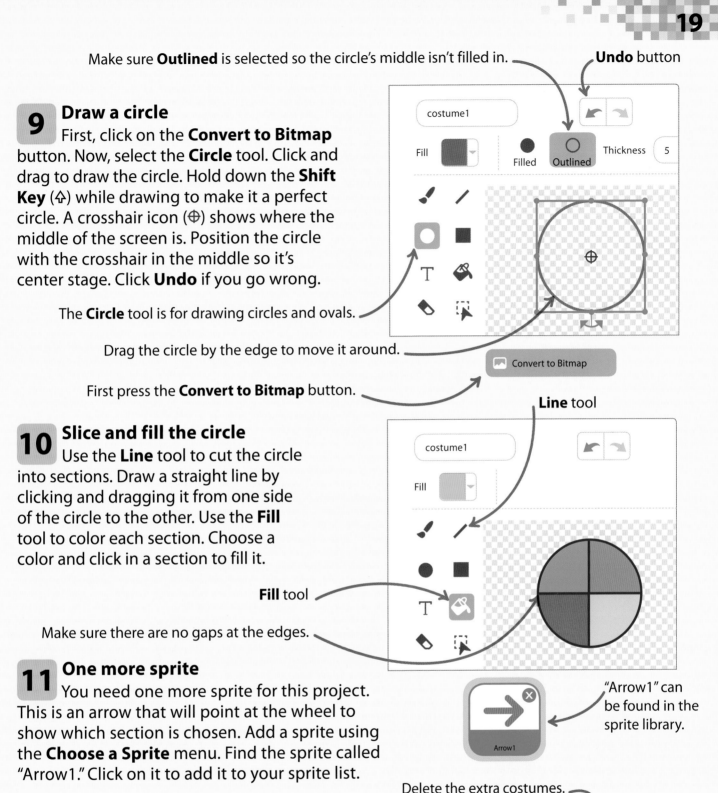

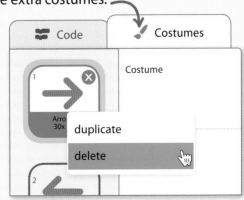

13 Edit the costumes

Scratch lets you edit costumes. Click on the costume with the arrow facing down. Use the **Eraser** tool to remove the sides of the arrow. It should end up looking like a pointer, or line.

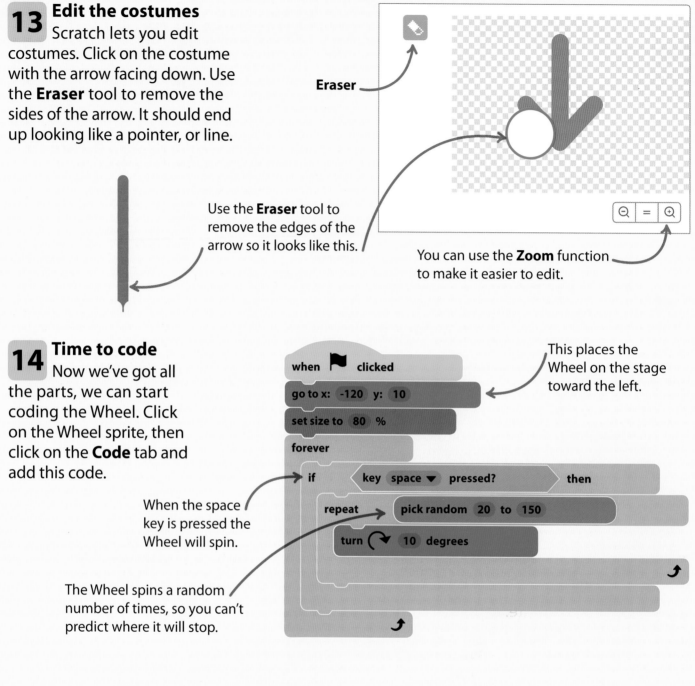

Eraser

You can use the **Zoom** function to make it easier to edit.

Use the **Eraser** tool to remove the edges of the arrow so it looks like this.

14 Time to code

Now we've got all the parts, we can start coding the Wheel. Click on the Wheel sprite, then click on the **Code** tab and add this code.

when ⚑ clicked
go to x: -120 y: 10
set size to 80 %
forever
  if ⟨ key space ▾ pressed? ⟩ then
    repeat ⟨ pick random 20 to 150 ⟩
      turn ↻ 10 degrees

This places the Wheel on the stage toward the left.

When the space key is pressed the Wheel will spin.

The Wheel spins a random number of times, so you can't predict where it will stop.

15 Add a broadcast block

Next, you need to use a **broadcast** block. This is a way to send messages between sprites. You'll find it in the **Events** section. Drag it into your code area, then from the drop-down menu choose **New Message** and rename it SpinStop.

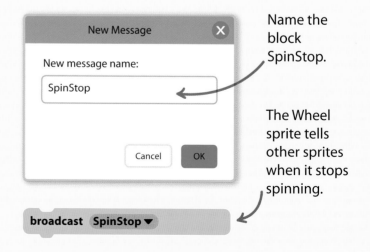

New Message ✕

New message name:

SpinStop

Cancel   OK

Name the block SpinStop.

The Wheel sprite tells other sprites when it stops spinning.

broadcast SpinStop ▾

16 **Add it to your wheel code**
Now add this block to your code for the Wheel sprite.

```
when [flag] clicked
go to x: -120 y: 10
set size to 80 %
forever
    if < key space ▼ pressed? > then
        repeat  pick random 20 to 150
            turn ↻ 10 degrees
        broadcast SpinStop ▼
```

17 **Code the arrow**
Click on the Arrow1 sprite. Add this code to position it. You might need to change the values (numbers) depending on the size of your wheel. Make sure it's in the right place, touching the wheel.

The bottom of the arrow should touch the wheel.

```
when [flag] clicked
go to x: -123 y: 134
```

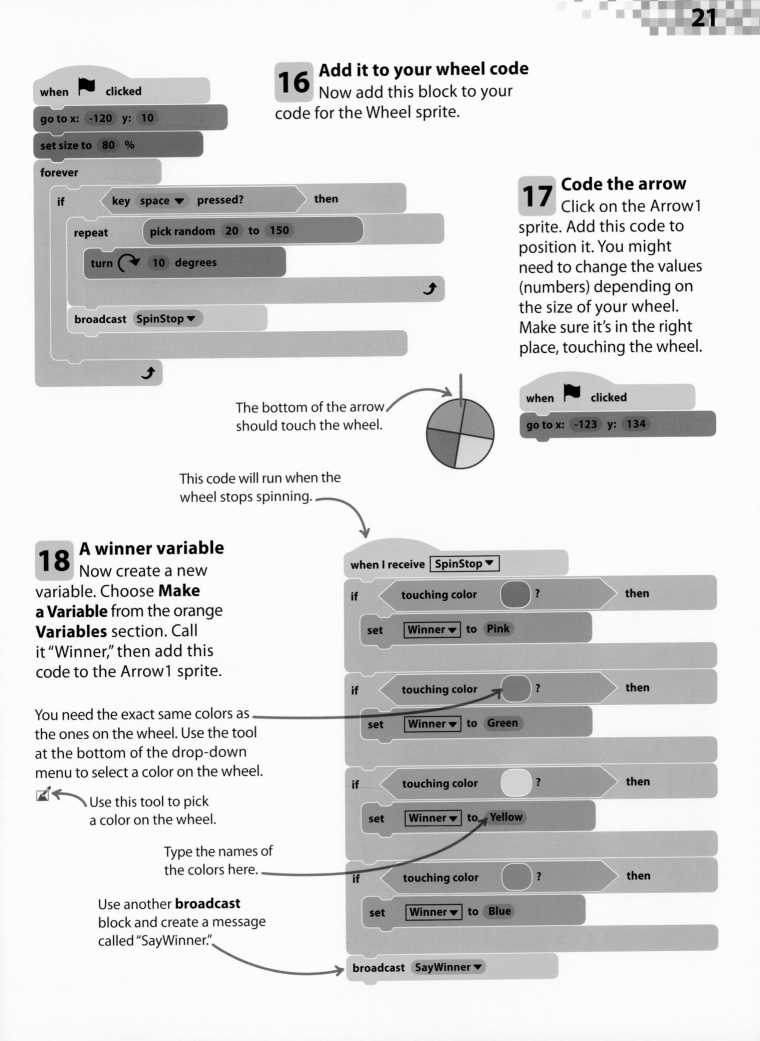

This code will run when the wheel stops spinning.

18 **A winner variable**
Now create a new variable. Choose **Make a Variable** from the orange **Variables** section. Call it "Winner," then add this code to the Arrow1 sprite.

You need the exact same colors as the ones on the wheel. Use the tool at the bottom of the drop-down menu to select a color on the wheel.

Use this tool to pick a color on the wheel.

Type the names of the colors here.

Use another **broadcast** block and create a message called "SayWinner."

```
when I receive SpinStop ▼
if < touching color [ ] ? > then
    set Winner ▼ to Pink
if < touching color [ ] ? > then
    set Winner ▼ to Green
if < touching color [ ] ? > then
    set Winner ▼ to Yellow
if < touching color [ ] ? > then
    set Winner ▼ to Blue
broadcast SayWinner ▼
```

19 And the chosen color is...
One more piece of code. This code lets Scratch Cat announce the chosen color. Click on the Cat sprite and add this code.

when I receive SayWinner ▼

say Winner ▼ for 2 seconds

This block can be found in the **Variables** section.

The cat says the name of the chosen color!

20 Try it out
Now you've got a working version. Try out your game by pressing the space button to spin the wheel. Check the code if it's not working as you'd expect.

21 Add video extension
Now let's get it working with the video motion feature in Scratch. This lets you use video from a camera in your Scratch projects. To add the video extension blocks, click the **Add Extension** button at the bottom left of Scratch. Then choose "Video Sensing." A new section of code blocks will appear.

Add Extension button

This lets you see the backdrop you've made on top of the video.

when ▶ clicked

turn video on ▼

set video transparency to 70

go to x: -120 y: 10

set size to 80 %

forever

if ◀ video motion ▼ on sprite ▼ > 10 ▶ then

repeat pick random 20 to 150

turn ↻ 10 degrees

broadcast SpinStop ▼

22 Update the code to use video blocks
Now click on the Wheel sprite to update its code. Delete the code that is currently there (right-click on the block then choose **Delete Block**), then add these new blocks.

Depending on your camera and the lighting in your room, you might need to change this number. Making the number bigger means you will need to move your hand more to spin the wheel.

This part of the code is the part that watches your video feed and can tell if you touch the Wheel sprite.

23 Time to spin
You did it! Get your friends and family to test it out with you. The wheel will spin when you wave your hand over it or touch it. Give it a spin!

Show what you know

1. Circle the correct words in bold in each sentence.

1a. The **start webcam** / **turn video on** block starts the camera.

1b. The **set video transparency** / **motion** block lets you see the backdrop over the top of the video.

2. Draw a line to match the icon to the paint editor feature.

Text tool

Fill tool

Eraser tool

Select icon

3. Which of these is not a font featured in the paint editor?

Curly   Sans Serif

Marker   Courier

4. Would changing the number from 10 to 30 make it easier or harder to spin the wheel?

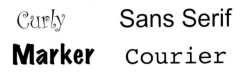

....

5. Try changing the number in this   ▐ set video transparency to 70
block of code to 100. What happens to the video?

....

6. Which of these blocks would
make the wheel spin faster?

turn ↻ 1 degrees

turn ↻ 0 degrees

turn ↻ 30 degrees

Challenge! Can you change the code to make the wheel spin in the opposite direction?

Scratch Cat Says

In this game, the player has to follow the correct instructions spoken by Scratch Cat. If you follow the wrong instructions, it's game over! Code this project and find out how to use the Scratch 3.0 Text to Speech feature.

Hear a chomp when this is clicked.

The octopus laughs when it's tickled.

Hit the drum to make a beat.

Click this to hear a ball being kicked.

▲ What you do

The player must click on the correct sprite after Scratch Cat says a sensible instruction. Get it right and the next instruction is called out. Get it wrong and the game ends! If it's a silly instruction, click on Scratch Cat. Following a silly instruction ends the game, too.

1 Let's go

Start a new project. You'll need to add four sprites for this game: Soccer Ball, Muffin, Jellyfish, and Drum. Drag and drop the sprites on the stage so they're positioned to match the picture on page 24—one at each corner.

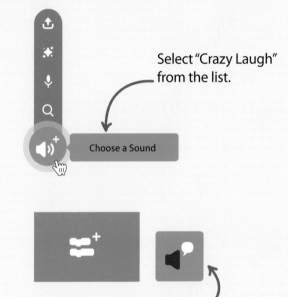

Add these four sprites alongside Scratch Cat.

2 Add some laughter

The sprites come with their own sounds, but you can add new ones. Our Jellyfish needs a laugh. Click on the Jellyfish sprite, then choose the **Sounds** tab at the top. Click on the **Choose a Sound** menu and search for the "Crazy Laugh" sound. You'll create code to trigger this noise later.

Select "Crazy Laugh" from the list.

Choose a Sound

3 Add Text to Speech extension

This game uses Text to Speech blocks. These brilliant blocks let your Scratch projects talk. To use them in the game you need to add an extension. Choose **Add Extension** from the bottom left of the **Code** section, then select **Text to Speech**.

Click on **Text to Speech**

4 Create a list

This game uses a special type of variable called a list. A list lets you store a group of items. In this game you can use the list variable to store a list of all the possible instructions Scratch Cat might say. To create a new list variable, click on the **Variables** section, then **Make a List**. Name the list variable "Instructions."

New List ✕

New list name:

Instructions

○ For all sprites   ○ For this sprite only

Cancel   OK

5 Adding to a list

On the stage you'll see a new empty list. To add an item to the list click the + symbol at the bottom left. Do that now and type the instruction "eat the muffin."

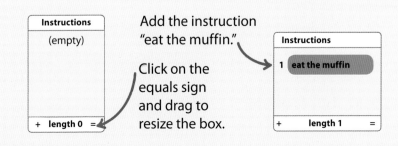

Instructions
(empty)

+ length 0 =

Add the instruction "eat the muffin."

Click on the equals sign and drag to resize the box.

Instructions
1 eat the muffin

+ length 1 =

6 More instructions

Now add these instructions to the list in the same way. The first four are the normal instructions, the last two are deliberately silly instructions to confuse the player.

Add these instructions.

Instructions

1 eat the muffin
2 tickle the jellyfish
3 hit the drum
4 kick the ball
5 eat the drum
6 tickle the ball

+   length 6   =

7 Another list

Now create another list variable. Call this one "Silly Instructions." In this list add only the silly instructions. Now you've got two lists: one with all the instructions (normal and silly) and one with just the silly instructions.

Silly Instructions

1 eat the drum
2 tickle the ball

+   length 2   =

These instructions make no sense!

8 Hide the list variables

You don't want to see the lists on the screen while playing the game. To hide them, uncheck the boxes with their names in the **Variables** section.

☐ Instructions

☐ Silly Instructions

Unchecked boxes don't appear onscreen.

9 Begin coding

Now let's start coding. Click on the Scratch Cat sprite and add this code. These green blocks are found in the **Text to Speech** section.

Remember you'll need to choose "New message" from the drop-down menu and then name it this.

You can select different styles of voice. Try **alto** for a higher-sounding voice, or **giant** for a very deep voice.

when ⚑ clicked

set voice to tenor ▼

set language to English ▼

broadcast Give instruction ▼

Set this to be your own language.

10 Pick an instruction

Create a new variable called "instruction." Next, add these blocks of code to Scratch Cat. This will choose a random instruction from the list, store it in the variable named instruction, and then read it out loud.

This is speaktacular coding!

When the "Give instruction" message is broadcast these code blocks will run.

when I receive Give instruction ▼

set instruction ▼ to item pick random 1 to length of Instructions ▼ of Instructions ▼

speak instruction

This is equal to the number of items in the list.

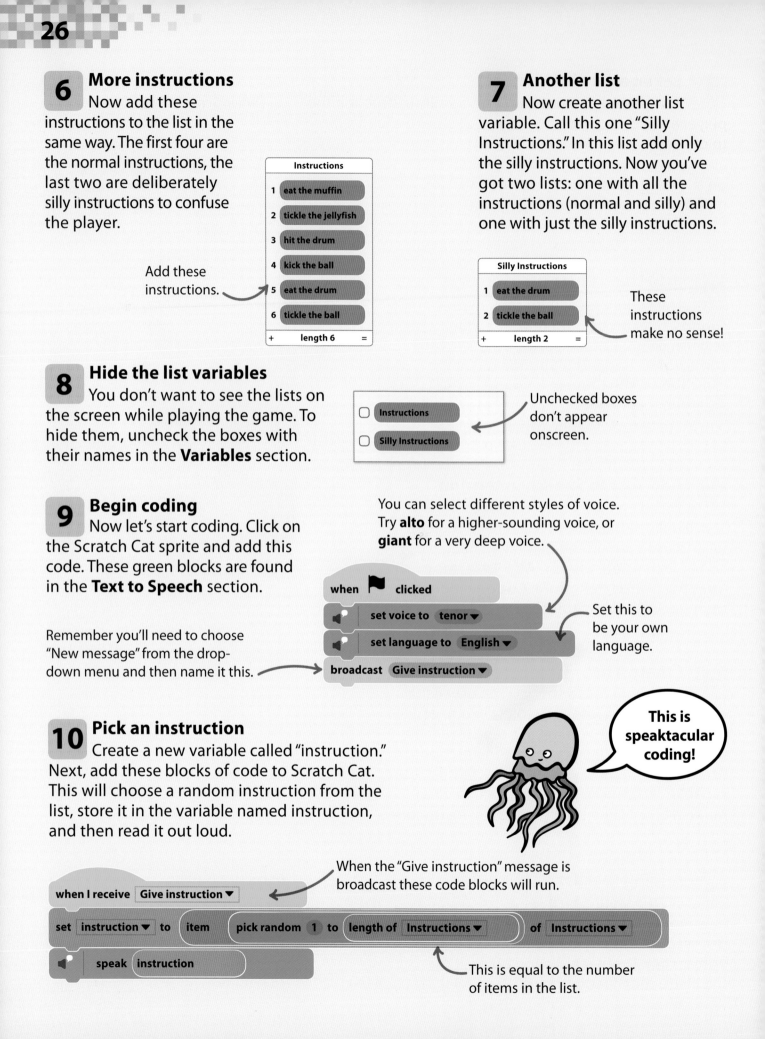

11 Is that a silly instruction?

In the game, if Scratch Cat says a silly instruction the player shouldn't do what he says, but should click on him to continue the game. Add this code to Scratch Cat.

When Scratch Cat is clicked if the current instruction is on the list of silly instructions, then get another instruction. If the player clicks on Scratch Cat after a normal instruction the "Game Over" message is broadcast.

```
when this sprite clicked
if     Silly Instructions ▼  contains   instruction   ?     then
    broadcast  Give instruction ▼
else
    broadcast  Game Over ▼
```

Create a new message called "Game Over." You'll write code to deal with this later.

12 Code the Muffin

Let's add code for the Muffin sprite—make sure you click on it first. In the game, when the player clicks on the Muffin, this code checks to see if the current instruction is "eat the muffin." If that is true, then it plays the sound effect and gets the next instruction. Otherwise, the player has made a mistake, so it's game over.

This must be spelled exactly the same as the instruction in the list.

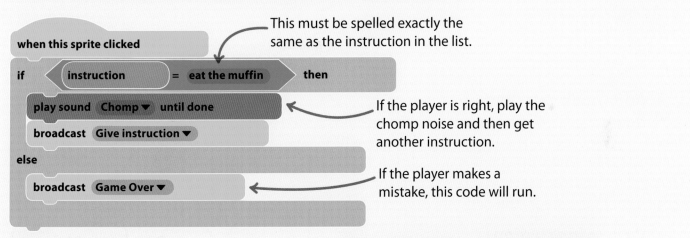

```
when this sprite clicked
if     instruction   =   eat the muffin     then
    play sound  Chomp ▼  until done
    broadcast  Give instruction ▼
else
    broadcast  Game Over ▼
```

If the player is right, play the chomp noise and then get another instruction.

If the player makes a mistake, this code will run.

13 Code the Jellyfish, Drum, and Soccer Ball

The code for these sprites is very similar. Add the blocks in step 12 to each of the sprites. Then, make the changes shown in this step to each sprite's code. The easiest way to do this is to drag and drop the code from the Muffin onto the icons for each sprite—this copies the code for you to change.

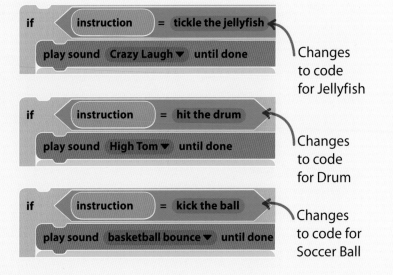

```
if   instruction   =   tickle the jellyfish
    play sound  Crazy Laugh ▼  until done
```
Changes to code for Jellyfish

```
if   instruction   =   hit the drum
    play sound  High Tom ▼  until done
```
Changes to code for Drum

```
if   instruction   =   kick the ball
    play sound  basketball bounce ▼  until done
```
Changes to code for Soccer Ball

14 Game Over

Finally, let's make one more sprite—a "Game Over" screen. From the **Choose a Sprite** menu, choose the **Paint** option. Use the paint editor to draw the new screen—you can resize the text so it's bigger and easier to read. Call this sprite "Game Over."

15 Add a sound effect

Click the **Sounds** tab and add the **Bonk** sound effect, or a different one, from the **Choose a Sound** menu.

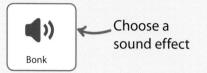

← Choose a sound effect

The **Undo** button lets you go back if you've made a mistake.

Bright colors will make it stand out.

Use the **Text** tool to draw the words.

Use the **Fill** tool to color in the background. Do this first.

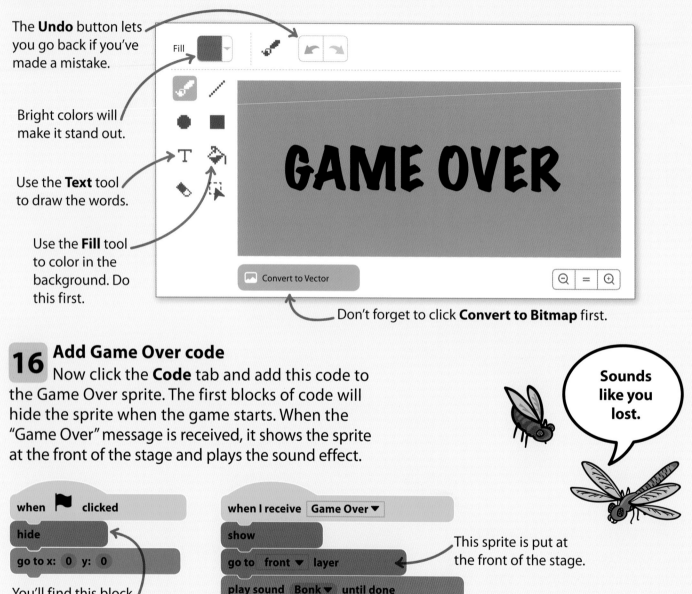

Don't forget to click **Convert to Bitmap** first.

16 Add Game Over code

Now click the **Code** tab and add this code to the Game Over sprite. The first blocks of code will hide the sprite when the game starts. When the "Game Over" message is received, it shows the sprite at the front of the stage and plays the sound effect.

Sounds like you lost.

```
when 🏳 clicked
hide
go to x: 0 y: 0
```

You'll find this block in the **Looks** section.

```
when I receive Game Over ▼
show
go to front ▼ layer
play sound Bonk ▼ until done
stop all ▼
```

This sprite is put at the front of the stage.

This ends the game.

17 You did it!

Now the game is ready to play! Have fun and try not to make any mistakes. You can always add in more sprites and instructions to make it more difficult, or add more silly instructions to trip players up.

Show what you know

1. Circle the correct words in bold in each sentence.

   1a. The **Text to Speech** / **vocal tool** blocks allow your projects to talk.

   1b. You use the **accent picker** / **set language** block to choose the language you want to use in your project.

2. Draw lines to match these voice options with their descriptions.

set voice to alto	**a woman's voice**
set voice to tenor	**high-pitched voice**
set voice to squeak	**says "meow" repeatedly**
set voice to giant	**a man's voice**
set voice to kitten	**deep-sounding voice**

3. The check boxes beside **Instructions** and **Silly Instructions** are unchecked. What does this do?

☐ Instructions
☐ Silly Instructions

....

4. There is a bug (a mistake) in this code from the Scratch Cat sprite. What is the mistake?

```
when this sprite clicked
if   Silly Instructions ▼  contains  instruction  ?   then
    broadcast  Game Over ▼
else
    broadcast  Give instruction ▼
```

Challenge! Make the game more fun by adding a new sprite and an instruction to interact with it.

Avoid the Asteroids

What you'll learn
• How to add multiple backdrops
• How to make a scrolling game

Pilot a rocketship through deep space, but watch out for the asteroids! This project shows you how to make scrolling games in Scratch, complete with a laser blaster to shoot the rocks and a scoreboard.

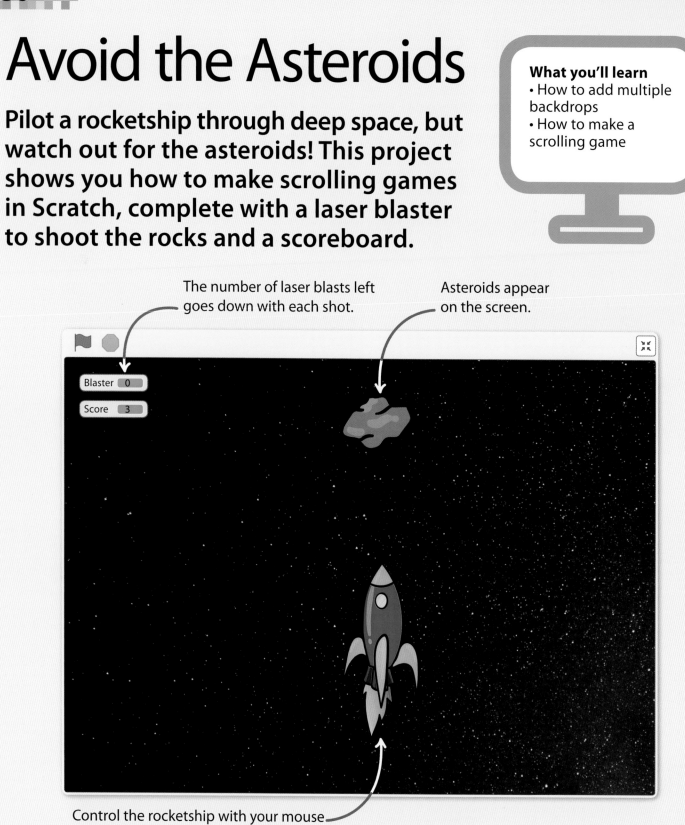

The number of laser blasts left goes down with each shot.

Asteroids appear on the screen.

Blaster 0

Score 3

Control the rocketship with your mouse and swerve out of the asteroids' way.

▲ What you do

Use the mouse-pointer to steer the rocketship through space, dodging asteroids. Be careful—more asteroids appear as the game goes on. The space key fires a laser to destroy them, but it's game over if the rocketship hits one.

1 Prepare for launch
Get ready for your space mission. Create a new project, delete the default cat sprite, and add sprites for Rocketship and Rocks.

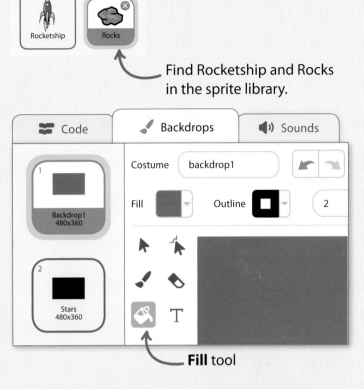

Find Rocketship and Rocks in the sprite library.

Fill tool

2 Set the scene
You need two backdrops for this game. First, click on the **Stage** section at the bottom right of Scratch. Next, click on the **Choose a Backdrop** icon and add the "Stars" backdrop. Then, select the **Backdrops** tab at the top left and click on the original "Backdrop1." Click on the **Convert to Bitmap** button, then use the **Fill** tool to paint it red. Click the "Stars" backdrop to select it as the default (usual) background.

3 Create all the variables
Let's create all the variables for this project in the code area. Remember, you do this by using the **Make a Variable** option in the **Variables** section. Make sure only **Blaster** and **Score** are checked.

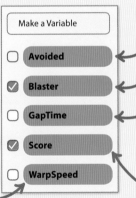

This counts how many asteroids are dodged.

This stores how many shots are left in the laser blaster.

This is the gap in seconds between new asteroids appearing. It gets smaller as the game goes on.

This is the player's score.

WarpSpeed is the speed of the rocket.

4 Set up the variables
It's time to code. Add these code blocks to the Rocketship sprite.

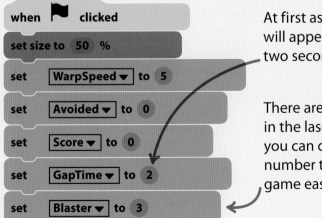

At first asteroids will appear every two seconds.

There are three shots in the laser blaster, but you can change this number to make the game easier or harder.

5 Rocket animation
Next, add this code to make the rocket appear as if it is soaring through space.

6 Steering the rocket

The player steers the rocket using their mouse-pointer. Add these blocks to make the rocket follow the pointer.

```
when ⚑ clicked
forever
    go to mouse-pointer ▼
    if      touching Rocks ▼ ?      then
        broadcast Game Over ▼
```

This makes the Rocketship sprite always follow the mouse-pointer.

If the rocket touches the Rocks sprite then it's game over.

Remember to create this broadcast message using the drop-down menu.

This checks to see if there are shots left in the blaster.

This plays a laser blaster sound effect.

```
when space ▼ key pressed
if      Blaster      > 0      then
    start sound laser2 ▼
    change Blaster ▼ by -1
    switch backdrop to backdrop1 ▼
    wait 0.05 seconds
    switch backdrop to Stars ▼
    broadcast BlasterFired ▼
```

This reduces the number of laser shots left by one.

You'll need to create a new broadcast message called "BlasterFired."

This quickly changes the background to red then back to the the Stars.

7 Fire the laser

Let's code the laser gun. When the space key is pressed the laser fires, if there are still shots left in the blaster. The backdrop quickly flashes to the red backdrop and back again, making it looks like the laser has been shot. Add this code to the Rocketship.

These blocks will update the score every time five rocks are avoided. If you make the number of rocks bigger by changing the "5" it will make the game last longer.

8 Update the score

Now add these blocks of code. They increase the score by one point every time five asteroids are avoided. It then reduces the GapTime (time between asteroids appearing) so asteroids appear more quickly.

The GapTime is only reduced if it's currently more than 0.5 seconds.

```
when I receive UpdateScore ▼
if      Avoided      mod 5 = 0      then
    change Score ▼ by 1
    if      GapTime      > 0.5      then
        set GapTime ▼ to 0.90 * GapTime
```

This reduces the current GapTime by 10 percent.

9 Coding rocks!

Now to write the code for the asteroids. Click on the Rocks sprite and add this code.

```
when [flag] clicked
set size to 22 %
hide
forever
    create clone of myself ▼
    wait ( GapTime ) seconds
```

Once the game starts, the forever loop keeps creating new asteroids.

This creates a copy of the Rock sprite, or a new asteroid in the game.

10 Flying rocks

The Rocks will move down the screen to make the Rocketship look like it is moving. They vanish once they reach the bottom of the screen. The **random** blocks are used so each asteroid starts at different positions at the top of the screen. That way the player can't guess where the next one will appear. Add this code.

```
when I start as a clone
set size to ( pick random 20 to 50 ) %
forever
    show
    go to x: ( pick random -240 to 240 ) y: 200
    forever
        turn ↻ 15 degrees
        change y by ( -1 * WarpSpeed )
        if < y position < -170 > then
            change Avoided ▼ by 1
            broadcast UpdateScore ▼
            delete this clone
```

The size of the asteroid is randomly chosen.

This places each asteroid at the top of the screen in a random position.

The asteroids spin as they move through space.

This increases the number of avoided asteroids.

This line is linked to the asteroid's position on the screen.

This removes any asteroid that hits the bottom of the screen.

11 Blast all asteroids

Add this code so that when the blaster is fired the asteroid is deleted. This means all the asteroids on the screen are destroyed at the same time.

```
when I receive BlasterFired ▼
delete this clone
```

12 Special effect sprite
We can create a special effect for when the Rocketship hits an asteroid by adding it in as a sprite. Choose **Paint** from the **Choose a Sprite** menu at the bottom right. Name the Sprite "Whoops."

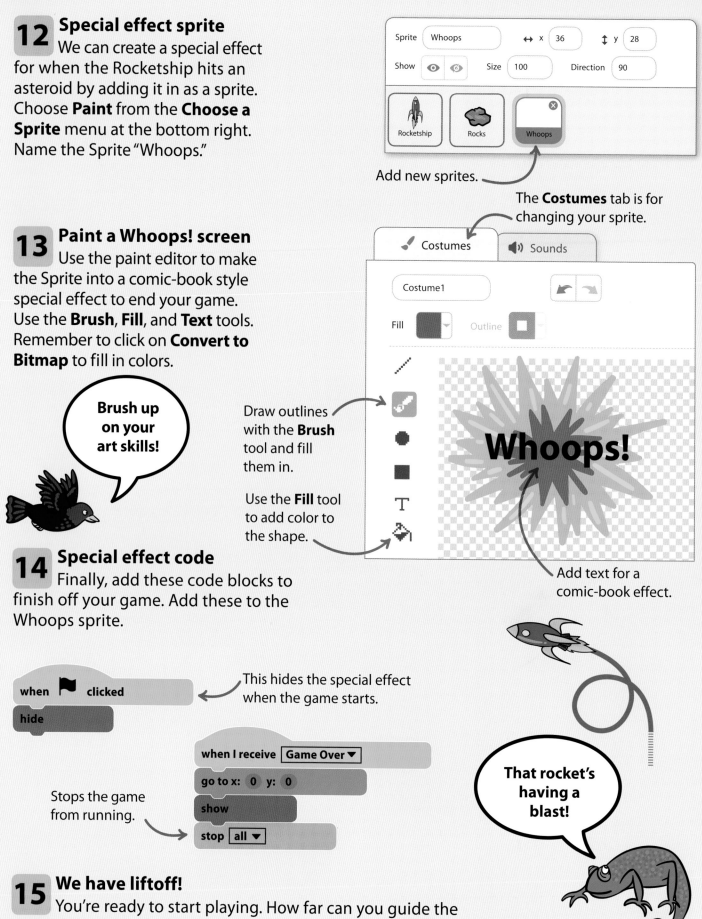

Add new sprites.

The **Costumes** tab is for changing your sprite.

13 Paint a Whoops! screen
Use the paint editor to make the Sprite into a comic-book style special effect to end your game. Use the **Brush**, **Fill**, and **Text** tools. Remember to click on **Convert to Bitmap** to fill in colors.

Brush up on your art skills!

Draw outlines with the **Brush** tool and fill them in.

Use the **Fill** tool to add color to the shape.

Add text for a comic-book effect.

14 Special effect code
Finally, add these code blocks to finish off your game. Add these to the Whoops sprite.

when ⚑ clicked
hide

This hides the special effect when the game starts.

when I receive Game Over ▼
go to x: 0 y: 0
show
stop all ▼

Stops the game from running.

That rocket's having a blast!

15 We have liftoff!
You're ready to start playing. How far can you guide the rocketship? Don't forget to use the blaster when you need to!

Show what you know

1. Circle the correct words in bold in each sentence.

   1a. The asteroids **move up** / **down** the stage.

   1b. This means the sprite's **x coordinate** / **y coordinate**

will **increase** / **decrease**.

2. Read each sentence and check the correct box.   **True**   **False**

   2a. The variable Blaster is set to 3 at the start of the game.

   2b. The value of Score is never changed.

   2c. The value of GapTime gets smaller as the game goes on.

3. What would happen if you removed this block then played the game?

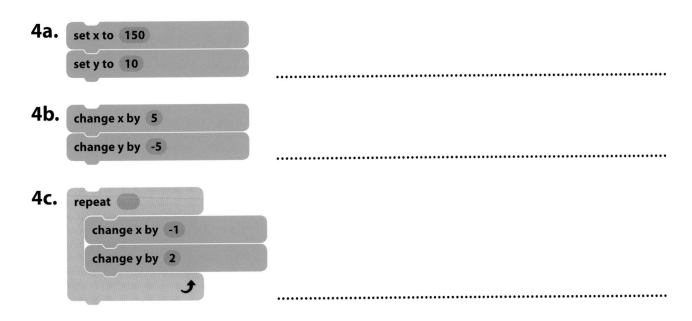

....

....

4. If a sprite starts at position (50, 50) where will it be after these blocks
of code are run?

  4a. `set x to 150`
           `set y to 10`

....

  4b. `change x by 5`
           `change y by -5`

....

  4c. `repeat`
           `change x by -1`
           `change y by 2`

....

Challenge! Try changing the game so that every time the score increases
the warpspeed also increases.

Solutions

You might have coded everything to perfection, but have you answered the quizzes correctly? Check your answers to the "Show what you know" quiz pages here.

Let's give them the answers!

pages 8–15 Unicorn Rush

1a. A (sprite) can move around the stage. It is controlled by (code) blocks.

1b. A (backdrop) is used to set the scene for each project.

2.

`change [Score ▼] by (5)`   Score is 5 (0 + 5)

`change [Score ▼] by (-2)`   Score is –2 (0—2)

`change [Score ▼] by (1 + 9)`   Score is 10 (0 + (1 + 9))

3. (90) is the number that should go in the empty window to make the sprite move to the right if the right-arrow key is pressed.

```
forever
  if < key (right arrow ▼) pressed? >
    point in direction 90
    move 10 steps
```

4. You would increase the number in this block to make the game last longer.

`when [timer ▼] > (10)`

5. The Unicorn would move quicker across the screen.

6. Set rotation style left-right

`set rotation style [left-right ▼]`

Challenge! To make the unicorn move slower around the stage you would have to decrease the number in all the blue **move 10 steps** motion blocks at step nine.

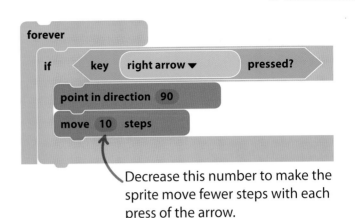

Decrease this number to make the sprite move fewer steps with each press of the arrow.

pages 16–23 Wheel of Fate

1a. The turn video on block starts the camera.
1b. The set video transparency block lets you see the background over the top of the video.

2. Draw a line to match the icon to the paint editor feature.

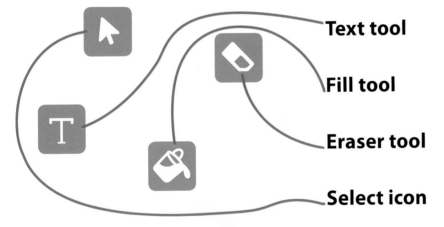

Text tool

Fill tool

Eraser tool

Select icon

3. Courier is not a font featured in the paint editor.

4. Changing the number in the **video motion** block from 10 to 30 would make it harder to spin the wheel—you'd have to wave your hand more.

5. If you changed the number to 100 in the **set video transparency** block, it would make the video fully transparent (see through), as though it's invisible.

If the number in this block was 0, the screen would be opaque (not see through).

set video transparency to 100

6. The **turn 30 degrees** block would make the wheel spin faster.

Challenge! To make the wheel spin in the opposite direction you would need to swap the **turn ↻ 10 degrees** motion block in step 14 for the **turn ↺ 10 degrees** motion block.

when 🏴 clicked
go to x: -120 y: 10
set size to 80 %
forever
  if key space ▼ pressed? then
    repeat pick random 20 to 150
      turn ↺ 10 degrees

Swap in this block to make the wheel spin the other way.

pages 24–29 Scratch Cat Says

1a. The (Text to Speech) blocks allow your projects to talk.
1b. You use the (set language) block to choose the language you want to use in your project.

2. Draw lines to match these voice options with their descriptions.

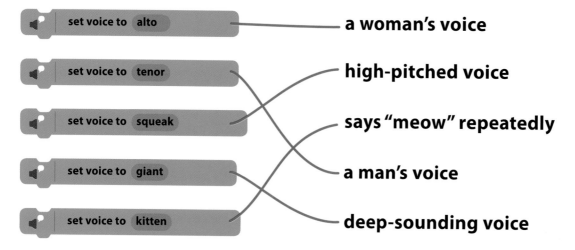

set voice to alto — a woman's voice

set voice to tenor — high-pitched voice

set voice to squeak — says "meow" repeatedly

set voice to giant — a man's voice

set voice to kitten — deep-sounding voice

3. The check boxes are unchecked because we don't want the instructions to show on the screen. The game would be easier if they did!

4. The mistake is that the **broadcast Game Over** and **Give instruction** blocks are the wrong way around. You need to swap their positions.

```
when this sprite clicked
if    Silly Instructions ▼  contains  instructi
      broadcast  Give instruction ▼
else
      broadcast  Game Over ▼
```

You need to put the blocks in these positions.

Challenge! Add a sprite, then make up a sensible instruction for the Instructions list. Copy the code blocks from step 12 to the new sprite, then change them to include the sprite's instruction and a sound that matches.

pages 30–35 Avoid the Asteroids

Show what you know

1. The asteroids (move down) the stage. This means the sprite's (y coordinate) will (decrease.)

	True	False
2a. The variable Blaster is set to 3 at the start of the game.	✓	
2b. The value of Score is never changed.		✓
2c. The value of GapTime gets smaller as the game goes on.	✓	

3. If you removed the **change Blaster by –1** block the blaster would never run out of shots because the variable would never decrease.

4a. (150, 10)   **4b**. (55, 45)   **4c.** (40, 70)

Challenge! Add this block to the code in step eight to make the WarpSpeed increase every time the score does.

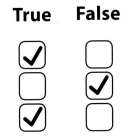

Add this block

```
change    Score ▼ by  1
change    WarpSpeed ▼ by  1
if        GapTime              > 0.5       then
```

Getting Scratch 3.0

You can use Scratch on the Scratch 3.0 website, or download a version that lets you work on your projects offline (without the Internet).

Scratch 3.0 is easier to use with a mouse than a touchpad.

Online Scratch

The quickest way to get started with Scratch 3.0 is using the online version. You can also share projects with your friends using the website.

1 Make sure you've got permission from an adult with an email address before you sign up for Scratch 3.0. Go to **scratch.mit.edu** and select **Join Scratch**. You'll need to make up a username and password. Do not use your real name as your username.

2 After you've signed up, click **Create** at the top of the screen to start a blank project. Let's start coding!

Scratch Desktop

If you aren't always able to get online, or you want to code offline, you'll need to install Scratch Desktop on your computer.

1 For the offline version of Scratch 3.0 , go to **scratch.mit. edu/download** and follow the instructions. The Scratch 3.0 symbol should then appear on your desktop.

2 To run Scratch 3.0, double-click on the **Scratch** symbol. Unlike the online version, offline Scratch 3.0 doesn't save automatically, so it's best to save your work often while you're doing it.

Note for parents

The Scratch 3.0 website is run by the Massachusetts Institute of Technology (MIT). It is intended to be safe for children to use. The instructions in this book are for Scratch 3.0, not the older versions of Scratch. The online version of Scratch 3.0 works well on Chrome, Edge, Firefox, Safari, Mobile Chrome, and Mobile Safari. Internet Explorer is not supported. Scratch Desktop works well on Windows and macOS. Help your child work logically through any coding difficulties. Check for common errors, such as swapping similar code blocks, and make sure that code blocks are controlling the correct sprites. Remember: coding should be fun!